Act,ONE

Act, ONE

C.C. Cervantes Dunn

Wordbinders Publishing

Colorado

Wordbinders Publishing
An imprint of Journey Institute Press,
a division of 50 in 52 Journey, Inc.
journeyinstitutepress.org

Library of Congress Control Number: 2023944215

Names: Dunn, C.C. Cervantes
Title: Act,ONE
Description: Colorado: Wordbinders Publishing, 2023
Identifiers: ISBN 979-8-9886470-1-0 (hardcover)
Subjects: BISAC: POETRY / LGBTQ+ |
YOUNG ADULT FICTION / Poetry |
YOUNG ADULT FICTION / LGBTQ+

Illustrations by: Emma Campbell

First Edition

Printed in the United States of America

1 2 3 4 5 6 7 8 9 10

This book was typeset in Fraset / Times New Roman

To everyone who has felt alone.

I hope this becomes a home for all those who feel lost.

And remember, you will always have a place on this Earth.

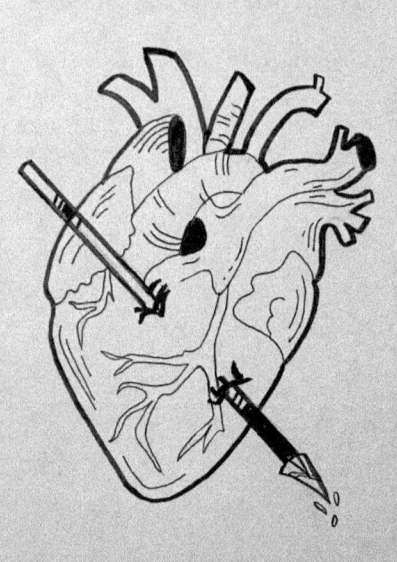

To Whoever Is Reading This

May I ask you why?

Why did you pick this?

Why this book

With this specific cover

This title?

Was it the words

Lining that made up

An ambiguous face?

Or was it the name

Firmly in its place?

Please tell me

Why you picked this book?

Is it because you can see

The pain

Blood

Sweat

Tears

That the words are crafted in?

Is it because

You can tell the words

Were written in blood

Dripping from my palm

—an aftereffect

Of a cut from a rose thorn—

Instead of the pen

To which

You've grown accustomed.

Tell me

Reader.

Please, I'm dying to know.

Because the blood

Is still dripping from my palm

And staining a once-white rose

Red

Instead of ichor gold.

Ask yourself "why,"

Before you trip into these pages.

Caught unaware

Of the words held within.

Because they have all

Been written in blood

From open wounds,

And behind some of them

A darkness looms.

But these words so tend to stain

The heart

With words

Meant to be imprinted onto a soul.

This is not a game.

These are words

Written in liquid rose petals

Instead of black ink

Shoved from a machine.

Contents

ILLUSTRATIONS

Preface

I understand that this is a strange place to pause–most authors start their books with the prologue and jump straight in because sometimes we just can't wait to start sharing the stories that have lived inside of us for so long. But I wanted you to read one of my poems before I started talking to you. Maybe it was because I wanted to use the poem as a hook. Maybe it was because I wanted you to know what you were getting into before I explained why this book is important to me. Or, maybe, it was because I wanted to share with you a piece of who I am—my soul, perhaps—before I attempted to reveal the rest of who I am to you.

Or maybe I wanted to give the English teachers something to mull over.

We'll never know!

What I do know is, I am happy you're here. Because that means you've made it this far, and I can trust you'll read the rest of what I have to say.

You are the reason why I wrote this book. You, my dear reader, are why I put these poems into a format that is easier to read than my messy cursive in a journal that has more coffee stains on it than my Speech and Debate scripts–and anyone who has had to deal with me can tell you that those are all but dyed brown from spilled lattes.

But I'm off-topic now.

I wrote these poems for myself, but I wrote this book for you. The poems helped me through dark times, and emotions I never thought would see the light of day. But I never wanted to keep these to myself. See, ever since I understood that I would have to become my own Wonder Woman, Iron Man, or Black Widow, I knew that all I wanted to do in my life was to help someone else. I never wanted to change the world in the same way my friends did. My dream was to help just one person. One person, because if I could help them, who's to say what they'll do in the future?

I hope I can help you, my dear reader. That's all I truly want.

And even if I don't, that doesn't change the fact that I wrote this book for you.

Delirious Dove

A dove,

The Greek symbol of love.

Aphrodite,

The symbol of beauty

Who can often act cruelly.

The two intertwined

Through an unholy design.

For the dove

Was often delirious

While Aphrodite

Was dead serious.

Love was the game she played

And the dove could not see

Her evil ways.

For she toyed with hearts

As if they were puzzle parts.

Taking chunks from past heartbreaks

And forcing them together

With another heart that aches.

But the dove only saw the beauty

Of the goddess

Who manipulated her sacred duty.

The delirious dove

Saw only the love

Of the goddess of beauty

While she stole his heart

And left him

When he fell apart.

She

Make it stop

Make it stop

Make it stop

Make it

"Stop."

"Stop,"

She says

And so I do.

Her hands grab mine

Forcing me to be still.

Her eyes stare at mine

Hoping

Praying

That she can see something

See something

And help me.

"Stop,"

She says again

Softer

Quieter

Firmer

Nicer.

That's when it hits me.

Nice.

She cares.

She is nice.

She is being nice to me.

She is helping me.

She

Wants

To help me.

And all I can ask myself is why.

Why would she want to care for something

I thought was broken beyond repair?

But here I am

And here she is

Crouching in front of me

Holding my hands

And staring into my eyes.

Solar Eclipse

I think I prefer it

When no one remembers I exist

When I'm just a shadow on a wall.

Not some once-in-a-lifetime

Solar eclipse.

Because then

There are no expectations.

No wants

From those around me

No one

To disappoint.

It would be me

And my shadow

Living as one.

Alone in the dark

Not sure what's to come.

And that way

I would never have to cry

Or smile

Or act like I care

Because no one would know me.

You see

I want to be like the air.

All alone in existence

But always around.

Something others rely on

But it can't make a sound.

I think it would be a beautiful thing

To be air.

Because then,

Whether they knew me or not,

Everyone would care.

Invisible

God,

I want to be invisible again.

I want to be able to walk through a crowd

And have no one notice me.

They might see me, sure.

A five-foot-five stranger

Brushing past them in the crowded halls.

But they wouldn't see me.

They wouldn't see what hides beneath the

Fabric

That covers my body.

They would see

The tears threatening to spill.

They wouldn't see

The way the book in my hands

Or the music playing through my earbuds

Was keeping me in that moment.

They wouldn't see

The pain wracking my body

As I wish I could trust someone

Anyone

With the pain.

They wouldn't see

The stupid agony I feel when she says

She can't make it to my birthday.

When she seems so indifferent

When I talk to her over text.

When, for a split second,

I think I'll be alone

When I turn sixteen.

I'll be alone in those theaters

Because all I wanted to do was see a movie

With three friends.

One can't make it.

One doesn't seem to care.

And one planned to be there

Until we had to change the day.

I want to be invisible again.

Because then

These things wouldn't hurt as much

Because I wouldn't have people to share

My sixteenth

Birthday

With.

I would be fine

Watching a movie by myself.

Because I wouldn't have invited anyone else.

Because I wouldn't have

Anyone else.

I miss being invisible, sometimes,

Because I always thought it hurt less.

Because I didn't notice the pain

Constantly weighing down my chest.

Yes,

I was lonely.

But it didn't openly affect me.

Why?

Because I didn't know

Until I had someone.

Someone who filled that empty space

Where the loneliness resided.

But when I feared that they left,

Left for good.

Left

Forever.

God,

That loneliness remembered the halls

Of my heart

Better than I remember the mental paths

I used to walk.

Being invisible was easier.

I miss being invisible.

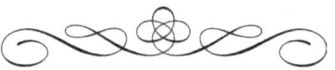

Truth

Someone

once compared my eyes

to melted milk chocolate.

Creamy and sweet,

and so easy to look at.

But my eyes

do not reflect who I am.

For I am not easy to look at.

I am hard

and sharp

and detailed.

I am bone

and blood

and skin that was shaped

with a sword

and sculpted with fire.

I am not creamy or sweet.

I am bitter and rough.

My truthful words

are honed,

piercing lies with stinging accuracy.

And my lies,

they flow off my tongue in ways

that would make a snake jealous.

My hands are rough with scars

from paper cuts

and my knuckles are bruised

from punches.

I am not creamy

and sweet.

I am not easy to look at.

Though my eyes may be.

See Me

I know you can't see it,

But I'm dying inside.

Some days are better.

Some days are worse.

But at the core of the days

I'm more dead than alive.

I know that

In reality

I'm more alive than I will ever be.

Twenty-two years old,

Right?

That's when the cells start decaying.

But sixteen?

Shit,

Your cells are just playing

Living their youth.

So to speak, at least.

But cell cycles or no

My heart is shattered

And the pieces won't let go

Of the tape and string

I've wrapped them in

Trying to keep them

From piercing my skin.

But instead my heart pulls

And strains against the bindings

Hoping that I'll get out of my own way

And see the pain I've been hiding.

Physically I'm fine.

I've always walked that delicate line.

But mentally I'm resigned

And emotionally . . .

Emotions are something so rarely dabbled in

The wondrous magic, all but foreign to me.

I cannot feel,

Half of the time.

It takes something great

Something sublime.

I know that the control is within reach

But I cannot grasp it

Unless I let myself off the leash.

I've tied myself down

To keep my shattered pieces together.

But that's only broken me more

Because I refuse to realize

That while the collar is around my neck

Taking away the breath I once longed for–

I was the one who put it there.

Because I thought it would be safer for me.

Selfish,

I know.

But I can't seem to let go.

And so I die a little each day

And each day a part of me drifts away.

Good Night

10

I know it's cliché

but I think about it every day.

Whenever my thoughts stray

I pretend to pray.

Because

9

my mind always comes to lie

on the bed I have made through years of delay.

All because I have never wanted to convey

my hate

for the place I am forced to stay.

8

Don't get me wrong

this is not about my home

or those I chose to love.

It's about the hate I have

for the safety of my mind—or lack thereof.

7

My mind is a mess

but I can't seem to express

my honest distress

when it comes to my minimal progress

and even less success.

6

What I keep telling myself

is that others have it worse.

Even when all I can imagine

is my body in the back of a hearse

or my ashes dispersed.

5

So time and time again

I pick up my pen

and write my pain

in hopes I'll forget my plan

and find a soft place to land.

4

I know it's not the answer

but if anyone asks

I leap around the topic like a prodigal dancer.

Because I'm afraid to cry for help.

Even when I know I'll be answered.

3

I should probably explain the countdown

as I prepare myself a barbed crown.

It's to keep me grounded

because my fear of floating away

is anything but unfounded.

2

And now that I'm going over the words I've shared

I'm realizing I'm unprepared.

All because this was my cry

my scream

and you're listening.

1

I believe this is when we say goodbye.

I hope I haven't made anyone cry.

Thank you for listening

and I'm sorry for my voice thickening.

I wish you all

a good night.

Le Vilian et Le Fantôme
The Villain and The Phantom

Il était un fois

> Once upon a time

D'abord.

> First,

Ensuite.

> Then.

Après.

> After.

Il n'y avait jamais assez de temps.

> There is never enough time.

Et on ne pouvait pas rimer.

> And the words never seem to rhyme.

Le prince est venu,

> The prince comes,

Et il a sauvé la princesse.

> And "saves" the princess.

Le méchant était emprisonné.

> The wicked are put behind bars.

Et les "héros" s'enfuyaient châtiment.

> And the "heroes" escape punishment.

Mais qu'est-ce qui s'est passé du vilain
                But what would happen if the villain

Il était plus qu'une visage terrible
                        Had been more than a terrible face

Qui voulait était connu
                                Who just wanted to be known

Au lieu d'été abducté
                        Instead of forced from the throne?

Il n'y avait pas la marraine,
                        There was no fairy godmother,

Personne ne veut pas ciller.
                                No one batted an eye.

Il ne s'appelait pas le roi du monde.
                        He was not called the king of the world,

Il était moins de l'ogre
                                He was less than the ogre

Il habitait aux frontières.
                                That lived on the borders.

Les années se passait
                                Years upon years

Et lançait eux-mêmes dans son chemin
                        Threw themselves in his path

Et il semblait comme si
                        And it seemed as though

Le royaume a oublié.

The whole kingdom forgot.

Oublié son triomphe

Forgot his triumphs

Et rejeté son plaisir

And dismissed his joys

Pour il était l'habitude de toujour

For he would always

Être la cible de toutes les blagués.

Be the butt of the joke.

Il souriait rarement

It was rare

Et le sourire sur ses lèvres

When the smile returned to his face.

Avait l'habitude de seulement apparaître

And the beaming on his lips

Quand il était entouré de fantômes.

Would only appear

Pour le fantôme n'était pas indifférent

For the phantom did not care

Si le vilain était quelqu'un à craindre

If the villain was someone to fear.

Tout ce qu'il voulait

All he wanted

Être pour quelqu'un à faire quelque chose
  Was for someone to do something

En plus s'arrêter à fixer.
  Besides stopping to stare.

Et de temps de temps
  And from time to time

Ils étaient tous les deux heureux.
  They were both happy

Pour le vilain n'était plus un vilain
  For the villain was no longer a villain

Et le fantôme ne se sentait pas comme un fantôme.
  And the ghost felt like no ghost.

Mais
  But,

Il ne pouvait jamais durer
  It could never last

Pour le vilain devait jouer le rôle
  For the villain must play his part

Dans le grand plan.
  In the great design.

Aussi, encore
  So, still

Comme les Parques décrétant
  As the Fates decreed

Le vilain est devenu le vilain
                    The villain became the villain

Et le fantôme était maudit par le roi.
                    And the phantom was cursed by the king
                                        .
Déjà
                                        Yet

Parfois
                                        Sometimes

Ils ont pensée d'avoir la tendance
                    Their thoughts would stray

De s'éloigner Jadis
                                        Back to those days

Où le vilain n'était pas un vilain
                    When the villain was not a villain

Et seulement un garçon.
                    And only just a boy.

I Tried

I tried to paint last night

And you know I have no eye

No talent for it.

But still I tried

In the wee hours of the morning.

And so,

I splashed the silver paint

Across the canvas

In a way I thought was beautiful.

But as I watched the paint drip

I saw that the silver

I had bought

Ran red

As if roses

Were cascading down the easel.

And so I thought

"I can never show this"

Because as I looked at the art I created

All I saw were slashes of paint

Across a board

Sloppily covered up

Under beige.

And so I hid it

Under black cloth

And denim.

Never daring to show anyone

The paintings I made

In the midnight hours

Under the light of the moon

With no eye

Nor talent

For brushstrokes.

And

You see

The paintbrush became a knife

And the paint I thought

Was splattered on the canvas

Was blood

Dripping down my thigh.

Breathe

I steady my breathing

As my heart races

Pounding in the throat

And pushing on my eyes.

I steady my breathing

As my legs collapse under me

Straining under the weight

I have had thrust upon me.

I steady my breathing

As my eyesight tunnels

Focusing on one

And then none

And then just a blank screen.

I steady my breathing

And suck in a breath.

As I push my back straight

And my arms from around my chest.

I steady my breathing

As I push myself off the floor,

Pulling myself away

From that godforsaken drawer.

I steady my breathing

As I steady my hands.

Because nobody needs to see the shaking

Because I don't want them

To misunderstand.

I steady my breathing

And tell myself I'm fine.

Because at this point

I have to be

And the words work

Almost every time.

I steady my breathing

And straighten my back once more

Because if I was fine

I wouldn't slouch

When I walked through the door.

I'll be fine

I just need to breathe.

Breathe

And bear it–

Or is that word supposed to be grin?

Either way

I won't let the demons win.

I'll steady my breathing

Despite my racing pulse

And hopefully this way

I won't scare the adults.

I can hide just fine

Behind this mask of breathing

And maybe I'll survive this evening.

Childhood

I have lost my childhood

In a way

Seemingly instant

That hits me as I lie

On a bed

I wish I were made of clay.

Because then I would be able to mold it

And shape it

Into something more

Than I'll ever be.

You see

I have lost my childhood

With the snap of my fingers

And a realization

That at this moment

I could care less about Halloween.

Rather, I am overcome with the want

To become unseen

To fade into the shadows

And to work

Until my legs give out.

I am wreathed in desire

To sleep

Instead of watch scary movies

And plan the perfect level

Of costume creep,

I would rather dress in a bathrobe

And tell people "I'm tired"

When they ask

Than put in the effort

To put on a mask.

My childhood is gone

And with it

My ambition

My fire.

I want it back

And at the same time

Cannot grasp

Cannot grapple with the fact

That my childhood is over

And my adulthood has not begun

I am somewhere in between

But I know I am nowhere fun.

Take me to the times

When a witch's dress would do

When all I needed

Was a friend or two

To haunt the night with

As we aimed to scare our way

Into bags full of candies and sweets.

Take me back

To a time when costumes

Were merely something

You could slip into.

And not something you wore

Day in and day out.

When it was only one night a year

You were something

You're not.

The urge

To go back in time

And slip on a costume

For what I now realize

Will now be the last time.

They're Not Just Books

I have such a terrible pain in my chest.

It feels like I'm breaking.

That the bird,

Masquerading as my emotions,

Is pecking away at my heart

And ripping at my throat.

It feels like it's taken my lungs

And used them for a cage,

Because my ribs were not enough.

And as I'm feeling this,

This terrible

Heartbreaking pain,

All I can think of

Are the books.

The books I gave you,

The one part

Of my soul

I can get back from you.

I can't get back my love

My care

My worry

Nor my time.

But the books,

The windows to my soul

That I so recklessly tossed at you

Praying you would handle them with care.

Those I can get back.

I can never get back,

All those hours I spent crying

Or worrying

Or simply thinking–

All of it over you.

I can't get back my love

That I threw almost as recklessly.

Or I would have,

If my love were not a slippery slope

That I myself fell down.

I cannot get back my worry,

All those times I was so scared

For you.

Of you.

I cannot take back my care,

Because my care is my love

And my time

And my worry.

I cannot get back

What you could never give.

But I will fight

With strength from hell

To get those pages back.

Not only because they are sacred to me,

But because I refuse

To let you hold on

To yet another part of me.

Promise

"I'm here for you."

I whisper the words

My voice tight and quiet.

"I'm here for you,

Always,"

I mutter

Wishing your tears away.

I know it's hard,

And I wish I could help more

Than whispering words

Through a receiver.

"I'm here for you,"

Is a promise I intend to keep,

Because it is the trust between us

That I don't want to break.

"I'm here for you"

Is something I say

As silent tears stream down my face,

But my voice steadies.

I clutch my chest

And suck in a deep breath.

Because I am here for you

And you don't need my pain.

I'll be okay for you

Because I'm here.

Here for your needs

And wants

And pleas.

I'm here for you

And you don't need to hear my tears

My fears.

"I'm here for you.

Always."

I promise them,

And I promise myself.

And as I drag the metal

Across my thigh

I promise myself

That I'll stay around

For one more day,

If not for me,

For them.

Because I said

I would always be there for them.

Today Was Great

Today was great.

No really,

For once I'm telling the truth.

The weather was nice

Warm enough not to need a coat

But also chilly enough

I could wear my new sweater.

See?

Great.

And I got to see my friends,

Which is always nice.

And I'm starting to like some of my classes

I think.

Yeah,

No, today was okay.

I mean

I'm in a little pain,

But it's nothing I can't handle.

It's just some backaches

And maybe a scab or two.

But that doesn't mean today wasn't okay.

It was fine!

The music in orchestra was a little hard

But nothing I can't handle.

I mean,

I wouldn't be in the advanced class

If it didn't mean something.

Right?

Right.

Of course.

Why am I second-guessing myself,

Today was fine!

I mean

Sometimes the smiles hurt

Or weren't as real as they could have been

But it's fine because

today

was

fine.

I'll keep telling myself that

If it can get me off the floor.

I'll keep telling myself that

If it keeps me away

From the one goddamn drawer.

I'll keep telling myself that

Because my friends need me to be okay.

They need me

To not be the one

Breaking down

Because they don't need to be the ones

Who take care of me

Every time I fall and scrape my knee.

I'm fine.

Because I have to be.

It doesn't matter

What my heart may think

It's my mind I need to believe.

And so

I'm fine.

Today was fine.

I'm fine

Just ignore the shaking.

I'm fine

Just ignore the lump in my throat.

I'm fine

Just ignore the coffee addiction

Or the new scabs on my ribs

Or the bruises on my arms

Or the rubber band around my wrist

Or the fact that I'm talking too much

Too fast

Breathing too heavily.

I'm fine.

I just

Need to take a deep breath.

I'm fine.

I swear.

I mean

Today was great.

Yes?

Someone asked

If I loved you.

And honestly,

I didn't know what to say.

Because

I mean

Maybe?

But I feel like it also might vary

From day to day.

Sometimes I look at you

And wonder.

Just

Wonder.

And, I mean,

I'm a writer.

So it makes sense that I would wonder

Because that's the bridge

My mind chooses to wander under.

It's not true

Because it's all in my head.

"But my dear boy,

It might still be real,"

As my oldest friend said.

But do you want to know

The worst part in this convoluted play?

I don't know

If I love you

Or not.

But I understand that

All I can do now

Is stay silent

And maybe say one day,

"I loved them,

But I let them slip away."

And maybe this is about you

Or someone I have yet to meet.

But all I know is

I'll always walk

Down the opposite side of the street.

In This House

In this house

We learn to respect.

Respect the parents

The elders

But is that respect reciprocated?

In this house

We learn emotions.

We learn to suppress our tears

And only show the smiles

Plastered on our faces

Like painted masks

On puppets.

Emotions are a choice

Not a feeling we cannot control.

We were born with your anger

And our mother's tears.

We were born from your blood

Sweat

And fears.

Why do you punish us

When you were the one

Who gave these to us?

We are not at fault

For something in our genes.

Me eroded away is love

Right?

Well that can't be true

Because you have beaten my edges away

For so long now that I

Cower

When you enter a room.

Cower

Not to hide but to pick up a rock

And beat you until

You have been eroded too.

I mean

It's not abuse

If your palm is open,

Right?

And besides

You've never laid a hand on me.

Unless we tallk about the handprints

That have been painted onto my thighs

From when you hit me and called it

Affection.

Tell that to the times

You've screamed at me

My sisters

Because we did something you

Didn't

Want.

So what if she bites her nails

So what if she still needs a hug from Mom

THEY'RE FIVE

They're allowed to be kids.

Don't make them grow up

The same way you made me.

Forcing me

To be the gifted kid you've always wanted.

I may not have played a sport

But I academically lettered.

I may not have been happy

But I aced all of my classes.

I don't have depression because of that

Right?

I mean

I can't have a chemical

Imbalance in my brain

Because I'm always smiling

Right?

You put the imbalance in my brain.

Mom did too.

Because it's hereditary

And something I cannot avoid.

So please tell me

Why in this house

We learn to respect.

Respect the parents

The elders

But is that respect reciprocated?

In this house

We learn emotions.

We learn to suppress our tears

And only show the smiles

Plastered on our faces

Like painted masks

On puppets.

But emotions are not a choice

They are something we cannot control.

You

Trust is earned

As is respect.

And if they are given

They are passed with a price.

A price paints blood

Quietly on walls

Reminding the bearer

Of the gift given.

"I will not betray,"

The bearer had said

When they accepted the gifts.

But they must remember

The pain and strife

That would grace the giver

If the bearer were to smash

The trust

Or respect

As if it were glass.

Glass does not glue

Back together as cardboard.

The shards shatter

And the lines always show.

And if the glass

Once held water

Now the liquid leaks out

Because of the cracks

And holes

Left from the fall.

Glass

And trust

Are one and the same.

For trust does not care

If you feel remorse

For the giver's feelings toward

The bearer

Shall always be morose.

My glass has been dropped

By too many people in my time.

So the only person

I now freely give it to

Is someone

Who has given me theirs.

She holds the glass

With tenderness in her grip.

For she knows too

How it feels to have a chip

In her glass' lip.

Do not pretend

To understand

For our love was tainted

The first time you pretended

To let the glass fall.

With a laugh from you

And a tired sigh from me

I blindly turned away.

But the second time

It happened

You were not fast enough

And a shard broke

From the rim of the glass.

So filed by anger

That badly disguised my pain

I threw the glass

And yelled at you with disdain.

My love be damned

And the love

You claimed for me.

You never once cared

About how I fared.

You never once held

My trust

Nor respect

With the same emotions

With which I held yours.

So fuck you

And the respect you claimed

To have for me.

Because when I look

At the glass in my hands

All I can see

Is sand.

Night

I know

That we stopped talking

Months ago.

And I know

That I made the decision

To cut you off.

Because from my side

Of this untold story

You hurt me more

Than I may have hurt you.

We both scared each other

Cutting down through flesh

And touching bone.

And you claimed to love me

But I was never your home.

And I don't know

Whether

Or not

You still think of me.

And if you do

Whether it is laced

With disdain

For me leaving

Or pain

For a betrayal.

Or

Even

Still love

For the times we shared together

That still shine with the beauty of a dove.

But know

I still think of you

And even wrote you a letter

When your birthday came around.

And know

I still have the matching pajamas

Printed with white bears

And llamas.

And I still read the notes

You gave me

On my fourteenth birthday

Because they bring a

Melancholy smile

To my face

And a rush of memories

That send tears dripping onto the lace

Ribbon that you tied them in.

Know

Sometimes I want to reach out

Because for four years

You were my person

Even if

Deep down

I was not yours.

Despite the scars

And the cracks on the bars

That surround my heart

I still miss you.

I miss what we had

Because it was a beautiful

Broken

Beaten-down picture

That fit the two of us perfectly.

Until I grew out of the frame.

And left you behind.

Six

Six bullets on my tongue,

Six holes in my lungs,

Six pins in my heart,

And

Six needles in my arm.

My destruction

So beautifully placed

Making the scars

Look like butterflies in space.

Five bullets on my tongue

But seven holes in my lungs

Add three more pins

In my heart

And ten more needles

In my arm.

How long must I play

This dirty Russian roulette

Because the closer I am

To one more bullet

The more butterflies

I let down

By imprinting them

Onto my body

With no regard

As to whether

They want to be there.

Trust

Bullet holes in my heart

Puncture wounds

In my lungs.

I trusted you

With the gun

Made of roses

And I didn't run.

I handed it to you

With a smile

And a kiss

Because I trusted you

And took you off my list.

The list I had written

Of people to fear

Because I trusted you

For more than a year.

And you smiled

And took it from my hands

Then shot me

And watched as I fell

To my hands.

You watched as I bled

And screamed on the floor

But all you did

Was walk out the door.

I trusted you

And handed you my love

But you took it from me

As you held it

With lead heald in your glove.

I stared

As you left my life

Blaming me

For giving you the gun

When all you planned to do

Was run.

December 18, 2021 | 16:22

I'll be honest

I'm not doing okay.

I'm not fine.

I'm not dandy.

I'm not okay.

I don't care

If your allergies

Are "killing" you.

I don't care

If I sound angry

Or look tired.

I can't fucking feel

Right now.

And I don't know what to do.

Because all I really want

Is to talk to you.

But I don't want to be a burden

With the shit

I can't even explain.

So I hide behind my book

And the music in my ears.

Please

I beg of those around

Just leave me alone

So I don't have to make a sound.

Because I don't think I can

With the state I'm in.

So please

Just leave me

To my books

And palms wrapped in linen.

I can't fucking cry

But don't expect me to smile.

Because only one girl

Can make me feel something

When I taste this vile.

I understand

That I'm not good company

Which is why I hide

And pretend to not exist.

But please

All I ask is that you don't leave.

Because when emotions

Come back into play

I know I'll miss you

If you ever go away.

And when I can feel

Maybe it will be real

And maybe I'll know

That I'm not a burden

To those around

Even if

I don't make a sound.

And

My gods

Do I want to talk to her.

But I also know

Her life does not revolve

Around me

And my feelings.

So as much

As I want to share

And get a hug

Through my phone screen

I'll hide in a corner

And talk to her

When her words

Can bring a calm to my heart

And a smile to my face.

I'll talk to her

When I'm okay.

When I'm fine

And dandy

And can care

With all my heart.

About The Heart

To know our hearts is one thing. To know some-one else's is something else entirely. For knowing your own heart takes pa-tience and peace. But to know someone else's is to want to wade through the deepest of rivers for a sliver of information. To know the heart of another is to walk through flames and to touch the coals to know the heat of their mind and the pain lurking in their shadow. And to know the heart of another is to love the water you wade in and the way the flames lick at your feet and stroke your hair. Because it means that you can become closer to the one you care so much about. To know the labyrinth that is hidden in their thoughts and feelings. To know someone else's heart is to know their pain and their pleasure and to accept both. For both are them.

♥

Words Are Words Are Words

And I wish

That I spoke with more

Eloquence

On my tongue

And less rasp

In my throat.

But I can only regard you

Think

Of you

With beauty's pain on my breath.

You were the beauty

In the world

I had created to fit you.

You were the centerpiece

To a raging disaster

Painted

As less of a massacre

And more

Of a masterpiece.

And for a time

That is what you were.

Until I realized

You had stolen my words

And taken the last shred

Of articulation

I had used to justify

My humanity.

I had used the silver tongue

You ripped away

To build the world

In which you stood.

And so I wish for eloquence

And a voice

As clear and sparkling

As a rushing river.

But you took those

When you destroyed

What made me.

And so I will speak

With the rasp in my voice

Each word

Clawing its way out of my throat

And into your ears

Because

Damn it to hell

You will listen

After years of ignoring

The vital words I have to say.

Humus

You are my home

Rooted in truth.

The truth

In trust

And trust

In love.

You are my home

Rooted in words.

Words

Falling from the anvil

Of the wordsmith

And shaping words

The same way

You sharpen knives.

You are my home

Rooted in lyrics.

Lyrics that map a universe

And glide on a melody

That harbor the lost

And save the damned.

You are my home

Rooted in poetry.

Poetry that describes the soul

That is home to all

And no poem is too small

That hold up the walls

And break down doors.

You are my home.

You are rooted in truth.

In trust.

In words.

In lyrics.

And poems.

You are my home.

Hush

My love is quiet.

My love

Is a walk in a park

With few words tossed aside.

My love

Is reading

Side by side

For hours on end.

My love

Is extra marshmallows

In hot cocoa

And the muttering of

"I'm proud."

My love is quiet

Compared to others

Who scream

"I love you,"

To a crowd

And have hearts

Imprinted on their cheeks.

My love

Is a soft smile

And closed eyes.

My love is trusting

You're not wearing a disguise.

My love

Is words on a page

And coffee dates

And songs

That will never be played.

My love, to this world,

Is quiet.

March 11, 2022

I don't know

If there's anyone here

To hear this

And I don't know if they would care.

But please

Let her be okay.

I need both my little sisters

Not just one.

I need them to live long lives

And be happy for once.

And I know

There's an infinity,

A forever,

In every moment

And for everything in between.

But I want my sisters' forever

To last . . .

To last ten decades.

Please.

Please.

I don't know what more to say than

please.

I guess I'm at the badgering stage of grief

If that's what this is.

But my sister is still alive

And I want it to stay that way.

So please,

If anyone is out there

Listening to my desperation,

Let her be okay

Let both of them be okay.

Or if I'm just talking to the wind

And even if that is the case

I need to plead with the world–

Let them both be okay.

Please.

Icarus

Last night I dreamed of Icarus

As he fell from the sky

After making headway

With wax wings to fly.

Last night I dreamed of freedom

In every shape and form

Because freedom

Is something given, not born.

Last night I dreamed of fear

And the way it takes a toll

On the mind and the body

And the moments it stole.

Last night I dreamed of lightning

And the way it shakes the earth

Blinding and frightening

And I dreamed of the reverse.

You see

Last night I dreamed of Icarus

Careening from the sky

Heading toward the mountains

Where river nymphs lie.

And Apollo plays his lyre

In a way that sets some kind of fire

In the minds

And hearts

Of those who desire.

Last night I dreamed of Icarus

And his want for freedom

And I can see

Why Apollo wanted to meet him.

From a Book I Loved

They say

I'm a girl in pieces,

Beaten and bruised

And shattered on the ground

Like mirror shards

After a fight.

They say

I broke myself

Because of the scars

And blood

I have created and drawn myself.

They say

I'm a girl in pieces

Because I haven't found a way

To put the mirror

Back together.

But what they don't see

Is that behind

The shattered glass

Is art

Wrapped in linen

And covered in gauze.

The blood

I have drawn

Is the paint that I use

On the canvas of skin

That covers my thighs

And upper arms.

The piece

I have created

Was born of coffee-fueled nights

And adrenaline-dictated days.

The times when I could say

"I have no friends,

Yet bear no ill will."

And now I can say

With all of my might

"The painting is done,

I'm finished for the night."

I Love the Silence

I love the silence.

How strange is that?

To love the thing

That has brought so much pain.

Pain

When you can't scream for help.

Pain

When you can't

Articulate

The emotions so many others can.

Pain

When all you can do

Is sit in the silence

And suffer.

But I love the silence

And the peace it brings.

The peace

When the thoughts finally stop.

The peace

When the mirror doesn't

Haunt you.

The peace

That washes over you

Like a wave on the beach.

The silence

That once was my captor

Is now my friend.

But not in the way

That screams Stockholm.

In the way

That requires knowledge

Of your captor.

I understand,

Now,

Why the silence brings so much pain.

And for once

I'm okay

With sitting in the quiet,

Not making any noise

Not moving a muscle

Not glancing around

Not cowering in fear

Of what's to come.

Just sitting.

And listening

To nothing

And everything

All at once.

Roses or Violets? Which One Is True?

Why is it

"Roses are red

And violets are blue"

When violets are purple?

Looking at this

Feels like running in circles

Because it seems

Like I'm fighting with my own mind

Over what color a flower is,

As if I've gone blind.

I don't know

If it's the poem

Or society I'm fighting

When I say that violets

Are not blue,

As stunning as blue can be.

But rather purple

Like I thought everyone could see.

Or maybe

It's the romance

I'm fighting

Because it is pushed down our throats

And is often

The epitome of lying.

So tell me,

Why in the name of romance,

Did we change

The color of one simple flower

From the color

Of the almost-night sky

And hyacinths

And nocturnal birds,

To the color of waves

And the mid-afternoon sky.

Both are beautiful,

Yes,

But I do not want the lie.

My Love Language Is You

Your eyes

Are a midnight storm.

A collaboration

Between the lord above, Zeus

And the earth-shaker Poseidon,

To create a swirling

Frightening

Beautiful tempest.

Your smile

Is brighter than Apollo's chariot,

You are more handsome

Than even Eros,

Aphrodite's prize son.

Even the rays

Of Artemis's star maidens

Following her moon

Across the night sky

Have nothing on your shimmering

Glowing

Radiant grin.

I say all these things

Not having met you,

Face to face.

I say these things

Only seeing pictures

And hearing your

Melodious voice

And infectious giggle.

I say these things

Not being able to wait

To meet you,

To hold you,

To laugh with you.

I say these things,

With a smile

And a sigh

And a wish

For the time we spend apart

To fly.

My Own Snake Hair

The first time it happened

I was in the 5th grade.

I didn't understand

What was happening

Because I thought

I was being a good friend.

I thought

Because she told me

It's what friends did

As she pushed me to the bed

And told me not to move.

That went on

For longer than expected

And I couldn't get out

Of the trap she perfected.

The next time it happened

I was in 8th grade

In an alleyway

Hoping to get away.

It was a friend

Again

But this time I knew

When I said "no"

I was supposed to be listened to.

It happened again

And again

And each time she said

"This is what lovers do,

Don't struggle

Because I love you."

But it's hard to feel loved

When someone has finger inside you

While they're covering your mouth

As the fear inside me grew.

Time and time again

Over and over

Until my knees were blacked

And the skin under my eyes

Were blue.

I got away from them

That part I hope is truth.

But that doesn't stop

The parts I know to be true.

I never wanted to share

This part of my lore

But each time something happens

I am reminded of it more.

So here I stand

Tears streaming down my face

Begging Medusa

To bring me to her embrace.

Because the gods I begged

Did nothing to help

But she grew snakes

And wings

And I thought she could help me fix

My mistakes.

I keep coming back to this

And what truly happened.

And I can't stop myself

From fearing that it was all imagined.

But each time I cry

And shake

And forget my ability to breathe

I'm reminded

What is true

And what society wants me to believe.

So now I count them

First time

Second time

Third time

And more.

And remind myself

About what happened before the war.

Who I was

And who I wanted to be

And I hope

Somewhere

That person still lives inside of me.

Am I?

I used to be God's favorite

Eyes plastered to the sky

Tears streaming down my face

As I promise to never lie.

My knees would hit the floor

As you created storms

That force humanity to fall

To their knees, same as me,

In swarm upon swarm.

My hands stayed clasped

In front of my heart

As you created wars

That you claimed were art.

I used to be God's favorite

Until the questions started flowing

Like the wine his favorite son made

When he decided your line

Was worth toeing.

The questions destroyed

The façade of favoritism

As you glowered at me

To the tune of your own hymn.

All I did was ask

And wanted to receive

Because knowledge was power

Or so I had perceived.

But when you cast me out

Screaming with words made of thunder

I knew my rightful place

Was in the world under.

You see,

I used to be God's favorite

Until I saw the truth.

He was no God

And I could no longer be soothed.

His throne is built from lies

And the sounds of his creations

Being crushed as he cries

To his own heavens

As world he built dies.

He was no God

And I was determined to expose him for it.

So call me a Devil

And forget my name

As you forgot his

Because as he once was Yahweh

I was once his Morning Star.

And in his persona he finds comfort.

In the one he gave me

I shall find mine.

I was once God's favorite

Until I found my truth

And if that makes me evil,

Then I will chuckle and say,

"I was once God's favorite,

Until he cast me away.

But then I found my kingdom,

And shall rain hellfire on Heaven

To make him see

All the pain he pushed onto me.

And the people shall cry

"He made his own bed

Where we will force him to lie."

Moon

How do I tell someone

I want them to look at me

Like I'm the moon?

Not the sun,

For to look at someone

as if they are the sun,

Is to not truly see them.

It is to see them as something

Unattainable.

Untrue.

Masked in assumptions

And ideas.

I want someone

To look at me like I'm the moon

Because they can see me

And all my scars

And still call me beautiful.

Handsome.

Something other than okay.

Ordinary.

I want someone to look at me

Like I'm the moon

Because it means there is someone

Shining brighter than I,

I want someone to see me

As the Artemis lovers see the moon,

Is to see the center of attention,

Then me

Standing in the corner of the room

And think

"That one."

I want someone

To look at me

The way I see the moon.

Surrounded by stars,

Yet somehow still alone.

I want them to see

My sad eyes,

My fidgeting hands.

My slightly downturned lips.

And think to themselves,

"Who needs the sun—

So far away—

When such a beautiful,

Imperfect,

Someone

Is right in front of me."

Is This Love?

When I fall to ashes

My last thought will be of you.

Of your smile

And the way your eyes would glow

As a grin split your face.

The way your upper lip would lift

In a lopsided Cupid's bow.

When I fall to ashes

My last thought will be of you.

Of your eyes, ever changing,

A green

Or brown

Or even sometimes blue.

And the way they catch the light

At dusk and dawn,

When the sun is soft and kind.

When I fall to ashes

My last thought will be of you.

Of your hands

And the way they move

Swiftly over a keyboard,

Or how your fingers wrap loosely

Around one of your colorful pens.

When I fall to ashes

My last thought will be of you.

Of the way your voice sounds—

Melodic and true.

The way you sound when you're excited

At something newly learned

Or even just laughing

At whatever I said to you.

When I fall to ashes,

As I am bound to do,

My last thought will be

That I wanted to spend more time with you.

Silence Part 2

I crave silence

Like a drunkard craves his drink.

With a fury

And a will

Leaving destruction in his wake.

I yearn for the quiet

Like an insomniac yearns for sleep.

A restless

Hopeless

Dreamless endeavor.

I dart after peace

Like a leader thirsts after power.

With a distinct aura

And unyielding fists

Angry at the world around him.

I beg for stillness

Like a wanderer begs for a home.

With a quiet pain

And the fall of your heart

With every step away.

I want tranquility

In the way a siren wants a song

On their breath.

A love that builds

Over time

And doesn't disappear

No matter how hard I try.

I hope for the calm

In the way a reader hopes for rain.

A soft

Melodic need

That leaves them in beautiful pain.

But I am not a drunkard,

Running after my demise.

I am not an insomniac,

Chasing the sleep I will never find.

I am not a leader

With my arms outstreatched,

Grasping at straws that I will never keep.

I am not a wanderer,

As lost as I am,

My direction fleeting

And heart no longer seeing.

I am not a siren,

As much as I love song,

Because my melodies don't rest in lyrics

But I am thoughts, locked away.

I am simply a writer.

Looking for the right words

To bring this poem

To a finish.

Do I Miss You?

I haven't opened the text yet.

The last text you sent me,

As trivial as it was,

I can't bring myself to open it.

I keep staring at your picture

Small

And in the top right-hand corner.

The icon

Your smile

The constant unread message.

I write you letters I never send,

I dedicate these poems to you

I think

And stare

All because of you.

And yet

I can't open the text.

I want to say I can't let you go,

But that's enough of a lie.

I would say I don't want you

To see that I read it

But let's be real,

You've probably deleted my contact.

I think

It's stopping me from rereading the words

Worlds

We swapped late at night.

The pictures we sent

And the brief moment in time

Where we basked in the light

Of each other's lives.

And so

I won't open the text

Until I'm certain I can let you go

Without the fear of falling

Back down your rabbit hole.

Last Time ... I Hope

This is the
last time I'll write about
you. Last time I'll speak your
memory. Last time you'll take any-
thing from me. I loved you, Yes. And
perhaps love you still. But I love her
more than you ever will. This is the last
time I'll ever say goodbye because you
have broken my heart more than enough
times. So I'll tip my hat and bid you
adieu, and spare not a glance the next
time I see you. This is the last time
I'll speak of missing your touch.
Because you do not deserve
the memory of my blush.
You do not get to live
inside the beau-
tiful   places
in   my
m i n d
a n d
I ' m
c o m i n g
to terms with
leaving   you   be-
hind. This is the last
time I'll remember that
night with a smile because
I refuse to recall the way you
warped my mind and I'll only re-
gard you as vile. You do not get to live
in my mind, heart, smile, life. So take
your grin and take your laugh. Take your
voice vice and violent delights. Leave me
with my peace, by taking your malice.
I refuse to be put down, belittled and
beguiled. I refuse to be another
pawn in the game you refuse
to name, because finally, I
know who to blame.

Freefall

My love for you

Can only be called one thing:

Freefall.

I tripped off the cliff

And fell before you.

I broke my back

On the sharp rocks below

And was laid bare in front of you.

And here I still lie

Unbeknownst to you,

In all your godly grace.

Lying in a pool of love,

That looks too much like blood.

I lie here still,

Unable to move,

And here I shall stay,

Seen or not,

Unwillingly baring my soul

If only to you.

For You. Wherever You Are.

"Face the sun

And the shadows fall behind."

Those words are written on a card

Forever burned into my mind.

It's the last thing you truly sent me

Told me

Showed me.

It's the last time I felt as if you cared.

"It's just a burning

Memory,"

You wrote.

Hands steady for once in your life.

No lines veered off course

No words skewed to the left.

How much time did you spend

When we were already bereft?

"To each his own,"

You quoted with a mind that stands alone.

"But to thine own self be true."

I wonder,

With this,

Who you are talking to.

See, friends say this is how you let go

How you told me you understood,

But if that were true

Our friendship should have withstood

The pain and the sorrow

Of both of our lives

And yet you have left me,

Like Eros left Psyche.

But I stand here now,

Looking at the pen strokes

Embedded on this paper that will forever be locked away.

And I am at peace

For a reason I have yet to understand.

You were my world

But I was never one

To hold the world in my hand.

I see you from afar,

My ring still gracing your finger.

And I realize,

In your mind, I still linger.

I meant this to be a goodbye,

And a goodbye it will be.

But I don't think I'll ever

be able to put those words

Into adequate poetry.

So I'll hide behind

A mass of beautiful words,

Verbs upon verbs

And a way to hide what I want to be heard.

And so I repeat to you,

"It's just a burning memory,"

And say for one last time,

I hope you remember me.

Afterword

I was raised by an English teacher–my father–and I have always had an affinity for my English classes. And, though I've never fully understood why English teachers are so infatuated with the idea of deeper meanings in prose. Over the course of writing this book, I have been able to look at it from the perspective of not only my father as a person, but as an English teacher as well. And I surprised myself, to be completely candid; I started to understand their drive to find the deeper meanings. So, for my readers who love picking apart poems and novels, for my readers who don't want to put my book down yet, and for my English teachers who have taught me so much, here's why I wrote some of the poems in this book. On that note, I'd love to say that some of what follows was pulled from an email chain I have with my 8th-grade English teacher, the lovely Ms. Frahm. Ms. Frahm, if you recognize any of this, I promise I will cite you if I use any of your direct words. You taught me well.

"*Icarus*" was one of my favorites, if I'll be completely honest. And, truthfully, I don't recall knowing what I wanted to do with the poem, nor the exact inspiration. I will say, I enjoy the image of fighting for something you want so desperately, even if you know somewhere deep down that you'll never succeed. I do respect Icarus on so many levels because he knew what he wanted, and he was willing to go after it, even once he understood that he couldn't come back from his choice. The lesson on hubris is important, but I also think it's important to teach ambition and make it more okay to fight for something you want with all your living soul.

As for "*Delirious Dove*," I remember a line coming to me - something about pompous pigeons and delirious doves - and I wanted to use at least one of them in a poem. I thought the alliteration was the funniest thing I had come up with in months. I like the way a line or some kind of inspiration strikes me, and I roll with it for as long as I can. I lose track of the time it takes me to write, and that is when I write the poems I enjoy the most. When it comes to the rhyme scheme I use, it's mainly an accidental byproduct of an approach rooted in trying to find a natural flow to my writing. I just kind of think of something and go "that's good. I'll use that next."

"*Am I*" is another example of this writing process. I wrote it in Kentucky this past summer when I was supposed to be having an in-depth college conversation with my dad's cousin. The line "I used to be God's favorite// eyes plastered to the sky// tears streaming down my face// as I promise not to lie," came to me while my dad and his cousin were talking about growing up in the Catholic church, and I knew I had to run with it. I recently discovered that I really liked the idea of repetition at the beginning of stanzas. I also wanted it to be somewhat about religious trauma, as well as how humanity had condemned Lucifer simply because he leveled an accusation. All he did was ask a question, and it found that - and the response to that accusation - to be incredibly powerful and interesting. I have found that people often hide behind a persona whenever they can. And when that breaks, that person can often stay self-absorbed, but it hurts the people who trusted them.

"*You*" was one of my more personal poems because it was based on a conversation that I had with someone about trust, and how I had experienced people disregarding my trust in them for selfish reasons. I did really like the extended metaphor as well; I've always seen trust as something extremely fragile that's given with the understanding that you don't break it. But because it's fragile, it's really easy for it to shatter.

I wrote "*About the Heart*" with someone very specific in mind, but it shifted from the original idea I had. I originally wrote it for a good friend of mine, and it was supposed to convey how much I trusted her, and how valued she was to me. It turned into something more like "*You*" because of my past education when it came to other people's emotions and needs. The poem was supposed to convey that I didn't care how dark someone's mind could be; if they were my friend, I would be with them whenever they needed me. It turned into more of a love poem that reads almost like a Shakespearian tragedy because of my overly dramatic word choice. With that being said, I try not to embellish many aspects of my writing because I want it to ring true with as many people as possible.

Finally, I'd like to talk about the last poem in the book "*For You. Wherever You Are.*" I wrote this poem when I ended a relationship with someone who I thought would be a part of the rest of my life. At the end of our relationship, I asked him to return the books that I had loaned him– about 11 books. I also wrote the poem "*They're Not Just Books*" about him before he gave them back to me. I truly see books as a window to someone's soul because you can understand a lot about someone from the books they chose to indulge in. When he dropped the box of books off at my house, he also left a letter in my favorite book that I had loaned him, with the words "Face the sun and the shadows fall behind. It's just a burning memory. To each his own, but to thine own self be true." It was his way of saying goodbye, and this poem was my way of saying goodbye. He never saw the poem, nor did I ever intend for him to read it. But it was my version of closure that I didn't get from him when I needed it. Truthfully, most of my poems were written from that place: from a need for closure, whether it be from someone who I hadn't seen in years, or for myself. Forgiving yourself is one of the hardest things you can do, and these poems helped me take some of the steps toward self-forgiveness.

Acknowledgments

Since this is the end of the book, maybe it's surprising that I don't know where to start. I never really know where to start, but I thought that I would when I reached this moment. There were so many people who inspired me to write this book and so many more who helped bring this book to fruition.

The first group of people I want to thank are my many teachers who told me I could do whatever I put my mind to - even if the stories I wrote in their class worried them. I would like to specifically thank six of my teachers, even if one doesn't formally teach. My first thank you goes out to Ms. Jesse Cartwright, who was my fourth and fifth-grade teacher, who not only helped me understand math but also helped me grow exponentially as a person. Next, I would like to thank Ms. Angela Mayes, who helped to spark my love of reading in the third grade with the books *Wonder*, by R.J Palacio, and *The One and Only Ivan*, by Katherine Applegate. I would also like to thank Ms. Jessica Frahm, my eighth-grade English teacher, not only for letting my imagination run wild in her class, but also for letting me share my haunting vocabulary stories. I'd also like to thank my Speech and Debate coach, Ms. Megan McDowell, for pushing me to be my best in school and for supporting me throughout my high school career. And, to Madame H, my wonderful French Teacher who has also pushed me to be the best I can be, all while supporting me in any way she can, thank you. She is the reason why I got through my freshman year of high school, and you're the reason why I push myself. And finally, I'd like to thank Mr. Kevin Peterson, from the nonprofit Denver Writes, for humoring me over the past five years, and for bringing me into Denver Writes as an intern. Thanks to him and his dedication to making writing fun for young people, I have found the confidence to create this book.

Next, I'd love to thank the team that helped put this book together - I know for a fact that this would have never seen the light of day without you. First, I would like to thank my incredible publisher, Michael Jenet, and all of the Journey Institute Press for offering me such an incredible opportunity. I also extend my thanks to my editor Jessica Medberry for adding my small book to your long list of projects. I am eternally grateful to everyone on the Journey Institute Press team for making my dream a reality.

And here comes the fun part: I'd like to thank my family and friends for helping me to get here.

Dad: You have inspired me from day one to write and put my voice out into the world. If it weren't for you, I would never have considered publishing a book at any point in my life, let alone when I was still in high school. Thank you for your encouragement and your insistence on a good education. Thank you for raising me, surrounded by books and your never-ending pile of essays for your English classes.

Mom: You are one of the strongest people I will ever know - and we both know you got it from Grandma and Abuelo. Thank you for passing your strength onto me, and your ability to show the world who's boss. You're a grade-A badass, and now that it's in writing, you are obligated to never forget it.

Grandma and Abuelo: I love you so much, and I hope you never forget it. You have always been there for me, and I am forever grateful. Grandma, you have always told me that I could write a book, and I have - thank you for the constant reminders that I could. Abuelo, I know you wanted an engineer in the family, but that's what my sisters are for. I just want you to know that I am eternally proud of you for who you are, and I am so proud to be your grandchild. You both are sources of strength for so many people in our family, and you both have inspired me throughout my entire life. Thank you.

Emi and Eli: First and foremost, I love you both. You are both little spitfires who, even at 6, are becoming wonderful, strong-willed, independent little people. And I hope that you will never need this book. But if you do, know that you get an overprotective and loving older sibling who will help you through anything and everything.

Ella, Ian, Sophia, Molly, Emo, and Lorianne: You have all been incredible and impactful people in my life, and I could not be more grateful to have met you when I did. Thank you for sticking by me, even through my rough patches. I am a better person for knowing you.

Emma: Hi, Humus. I hope you know that no matter what happens next, I will always be by your side. You have made me a better person throughout my entire life, and you pushed me to follow the one dream I've had for as long as I can remember: publishing a book that helps those around me. I know we don't send each other letters anymore but consider this my last one to you: I adore you, and I always will. Thank you for being who you are. Here's a public promise to you, that our chapter will never end.

Sienna: I'll keep this short and sweet, because I know you prefer that. Thank you for being here for my entire life. You're the reason why I am who I am today. Thank you. I'm so glad we have known and supported each other for so long.

And finally, thank you to all my readers. You're the reason for this book. And I hope you know, whatever you're going through, whether it be now, in the past, or in the future, there are people who love you for exactly who you are.

ABOUT THE AUTHOR

Chris Carmen Cervantes Dunn is a Colorado author and TEDx speaker who is finishing out their high school career. Though this is their first book, they hope it is impactful to all who read it. They enjoy spending time with a good book, a cup of coffee, and one of their cats; but they are often found with their sisters, or their close friends. They work with the local nonprofit, Denver Writes, and participates in their school's Speech and Debate Team.

Journey Institute Press

Journey Institute Press is a non-profit publishing house created by authors to flip the publishing model for new authors. Created with intention and purpose to provide the highest quality publishing resources available to authors whose stories might otherwise not be told.

JI Press focusses on women, BIPOC, and LGBTQ+ authors without regard to the genre of their work.

As a Publishing House, our goal is to create a supportive, nurturing, and encouraging environment that puts the author above the publisher in the publishing model.

Wordbinders Publishing is an Imprint of Journey Institute Press, a division of 50 in 52 Journey, Inc.